権代敦彦

ピアノのための

無常の鐘

ATSUHIKO GONDAI
TRANSIENT BELL

for piano

SJ 1172

SCHOTT

ピアノのための《無常の鐘》は、第7回浜松国際ピアノコンクールの委嘱により、2009年11月13日から15日にかけて行われる同コンクール第2次予選の課題曲として作曲された。

演奏時間——7分

鐘の音は仏の声。
あの世とこの世の境界に鳴る鐘、
その荘厳な響と余韻は、仏教的無常観を伝える。
この世の儚さを告げ、盛者必衰の道理をそこに聴く。。

《無常の鐘》は、古来「無常の調子」と言われ、
鐘を鋳る際に理想とされた黄鐘調（おうしきちょう）を基本とした音構成。
鐘の一撞きで生み出される、「アタリ（衝撃音）」「オシ（安定した音高）」「オクリ（鳴り終わり）」
という響の漸次的な変化と、減衰から想を得た時間枠とによって、成り立っている。

ピアニストによって撞かれる鐘からは、
梵鐘のような複雑な倍音が聴かれ、
残響の行く先に、清浄に耀く「無常」があらわれるだろう。
同時にそこに、「永遠」「不滅」にしがみつく自我への警鐘を
聴く人もあるかも知れない。

——権代敦彦

作曲家からのアドバイス
和音のブレンドと、その濃淡をつけるために、また残響を聴き遂げるためにペダルを十分に活用すること。グリッサンド奏法（特に黒鍵）に於ける円滑な演奏と手指保護のために、手袋等の使用を厭うべきではない。

Transient Bell for piano commissioned by the 7th Hamamatsu International Piano Competition, was composed as an obligatory work for the second stage of the Competition, held on November 13, 14 and 15, 2009 in Hamamatsu.

Duration: 7 minutes

> *The sound of a bell is the voice of the Buddha. The bell that rings at the border of this world and the other world, its solemn reverberation and lingering sound, conveys the Buddhist view of life as transitory. It tells us of the transience of this world, and we hear in it the truth that all who prosper must one day decline.*
>
> *Transient Bell is composed of a sound formation based on Oshikicho (which closely resembles an A minor scale), which in ancient times was called the "transitory tone" and was the ideal when a bell was cast. It consists of the gradual change of three sounds produced by one strike of the bell and a time frame inspired by the fading away of the bell's ring. The three sounds are called atari (the moment of impact when the bell starts to ring and tone height cannot be identified); oshi (stable tone height where all notes ring at the same time); and okuri (the ringing ends and only one note remains).*
>
> *From the bell struck by the pianist, a complex harmonic overtone like that of a temple bell can be heard, and "transitoriness" might emerge, shining purely, at the place the sound is fading toward. At the same time, there may also be those who hear a wake-up call to the ego, which clings to "permanence" and "immortality".*

Atsuhiko Gondai

Advice from the composer:
In order to blend and shade the chords, and in order to make the lingering sound audible, make full use of the pedals. For a smooth performance in execution of the glissando (especially the black keys), and to protect the fingers, the use of gloves is recommended.

Abbreviations and Symbols:

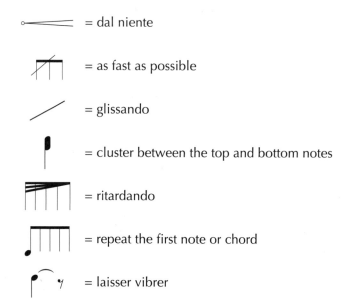

= dal niente

= as fast as possible

= glissando

= cluster between the top and bottom notes

= ritardando

= repeat the first note or chord

= laisser vibrer

Accidentals apply only to each note.

無常の鐘
TRANSIENT BELL
for piano

権代敦彦
Atsuhiko Gondai

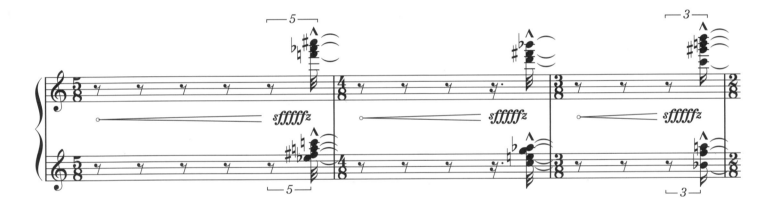

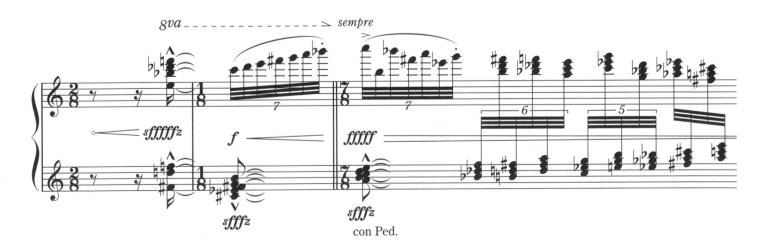

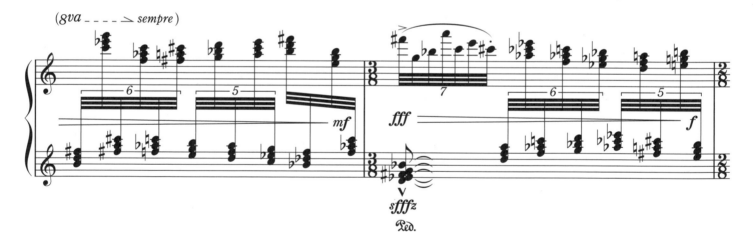

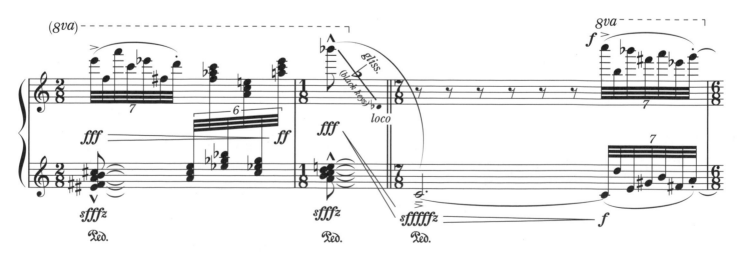

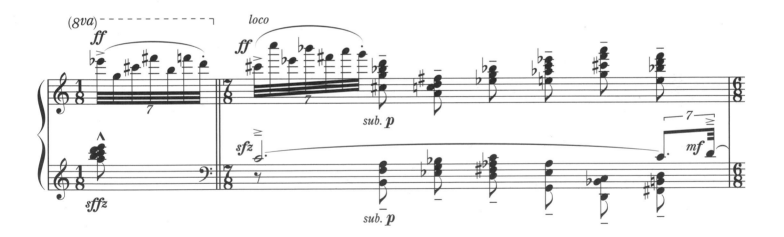

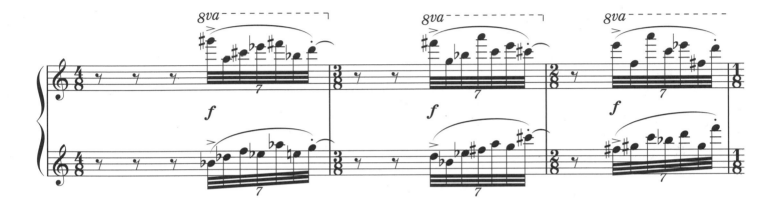

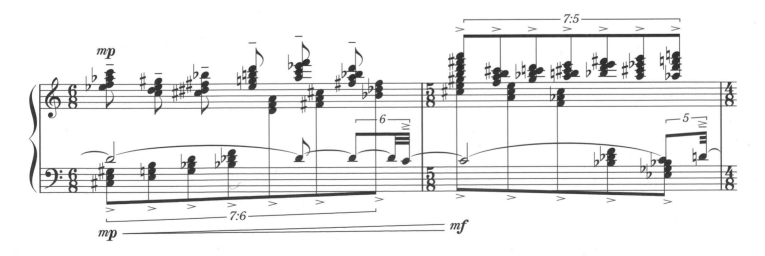

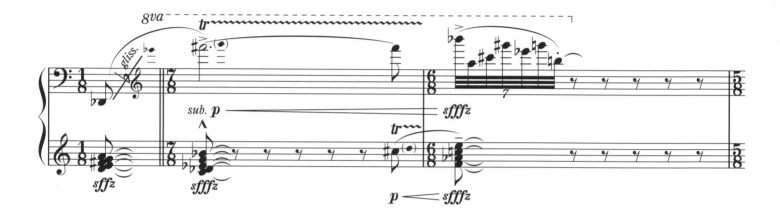

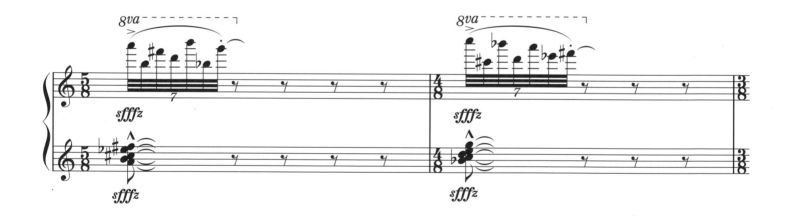

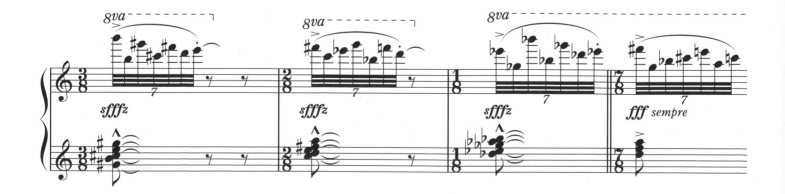

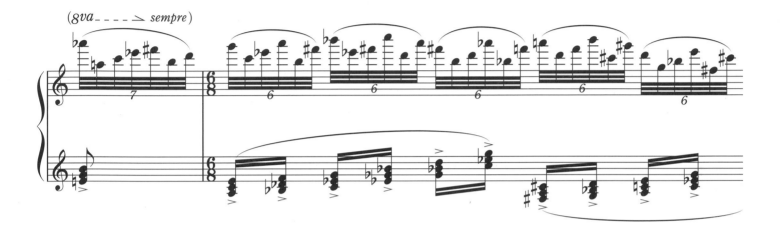

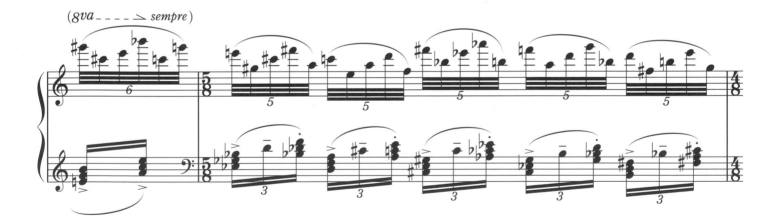

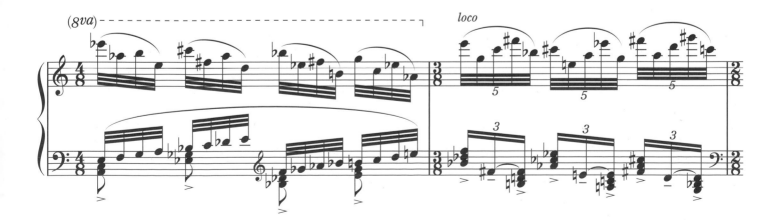

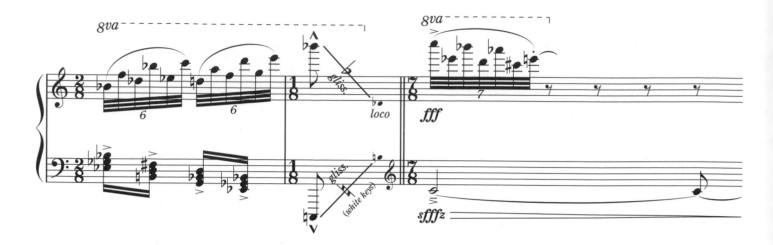

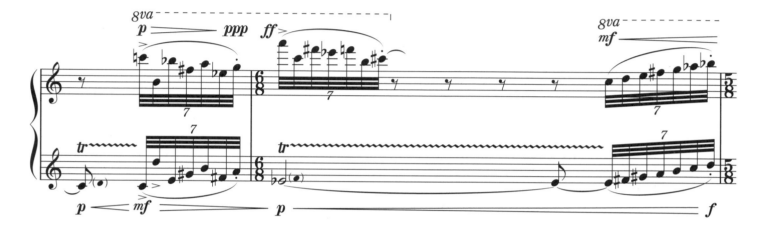

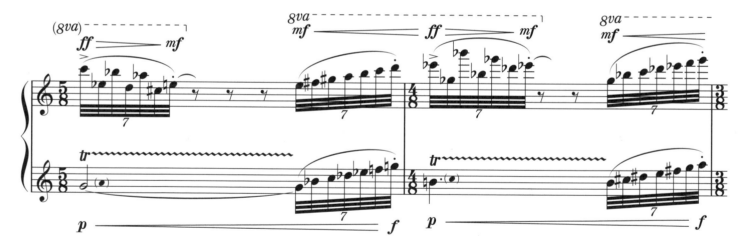

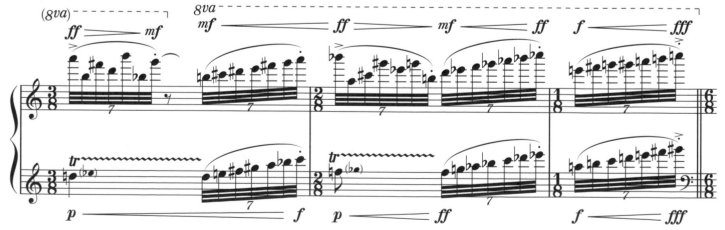

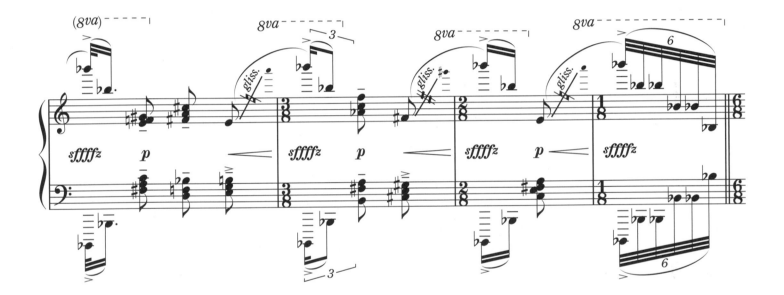

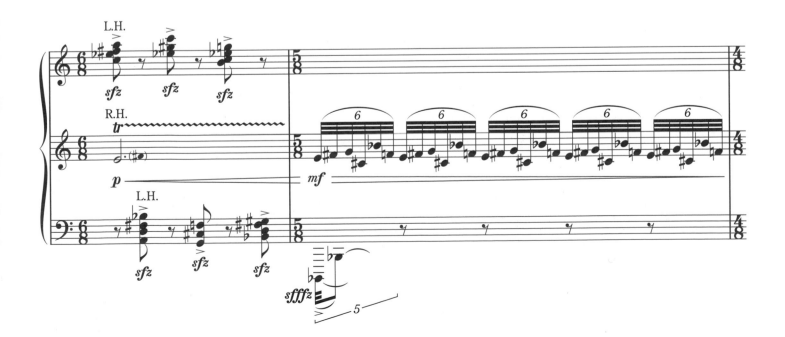

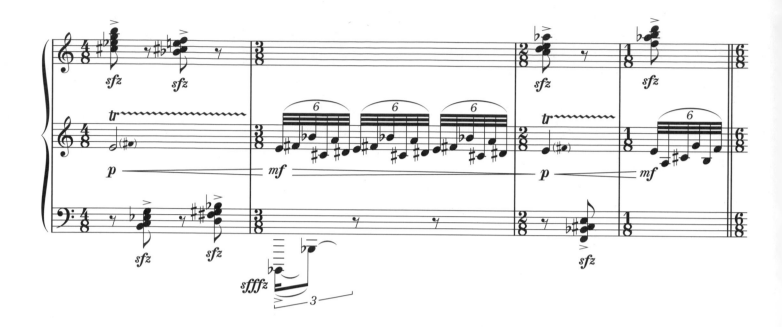

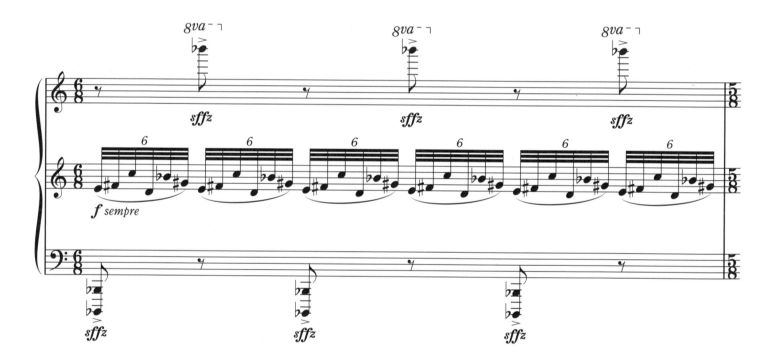

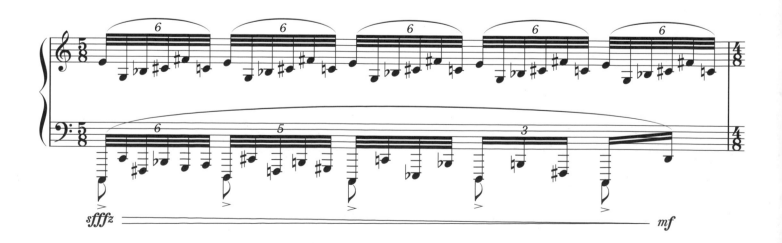

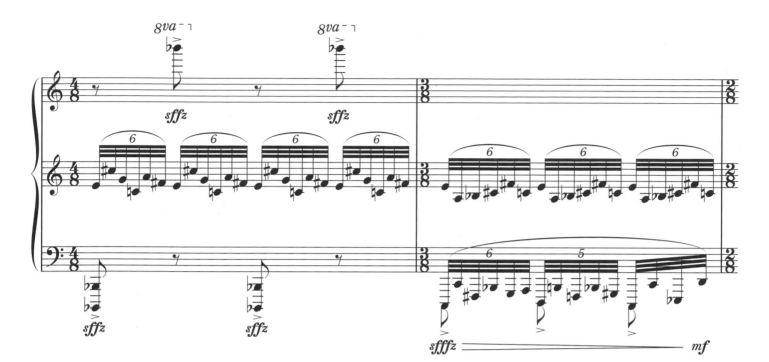

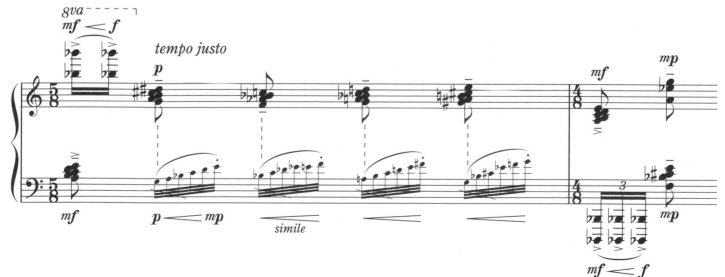

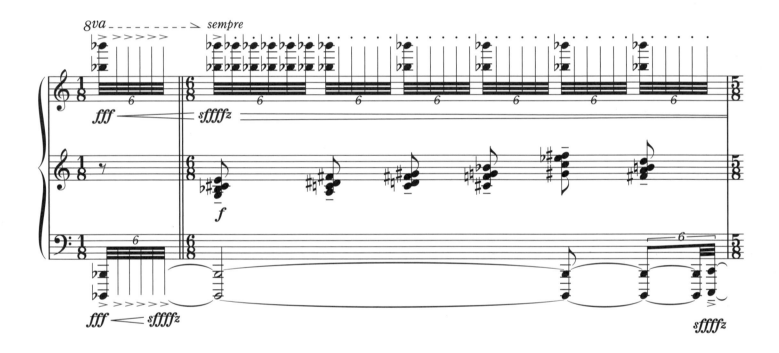

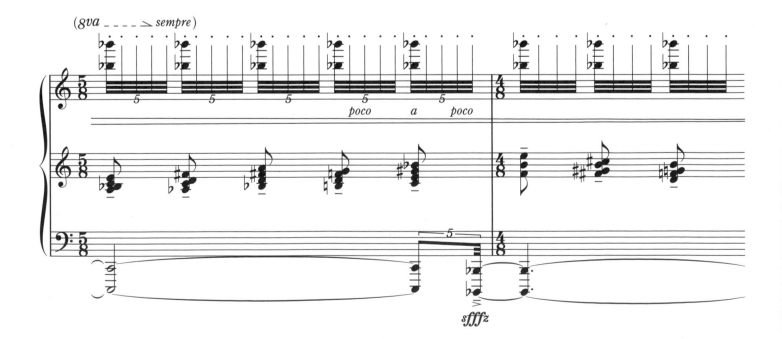

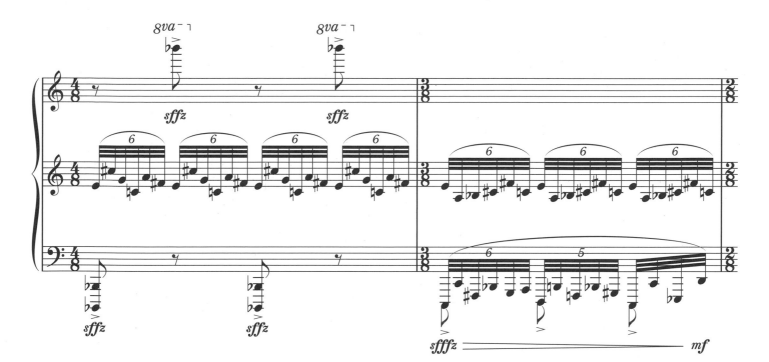

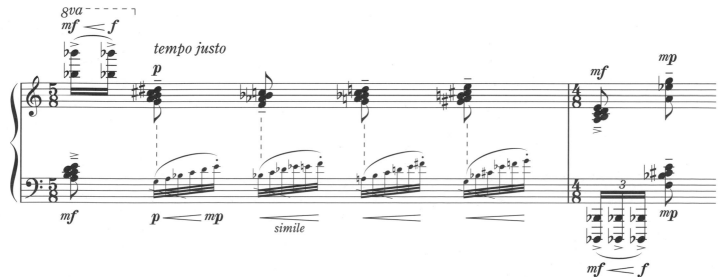

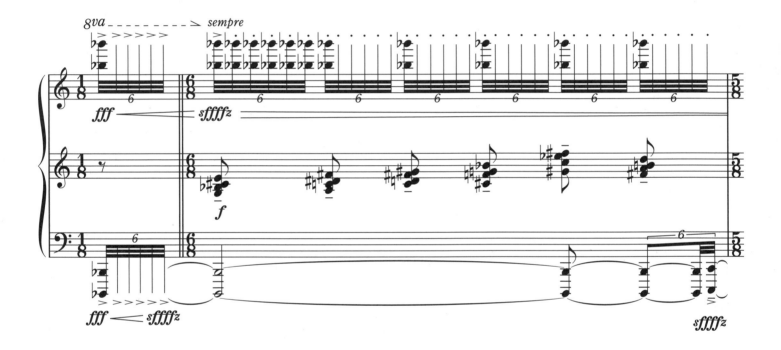

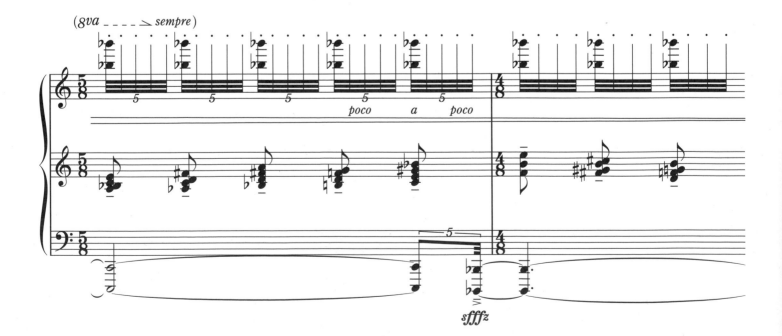

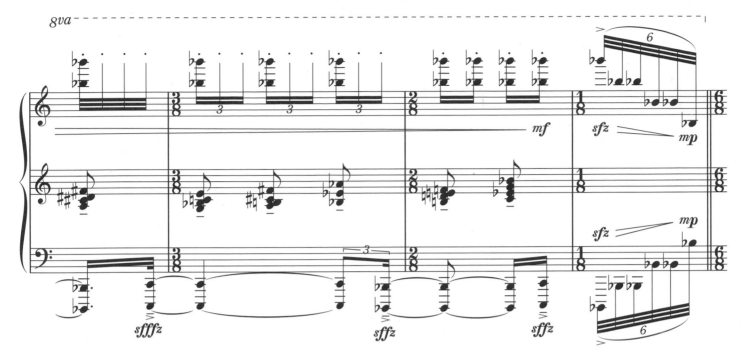

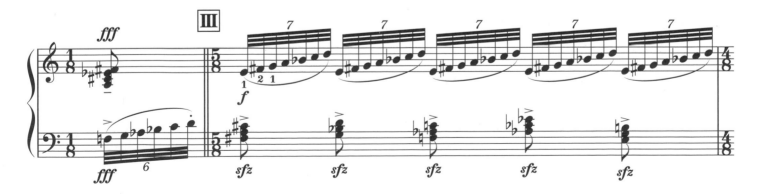

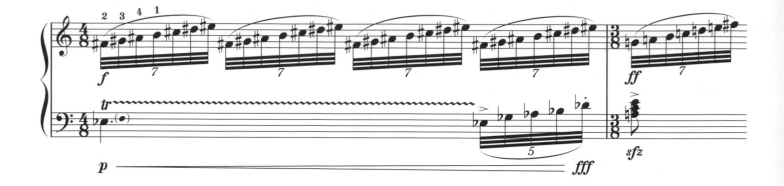

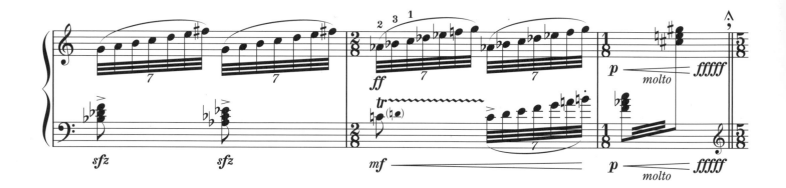

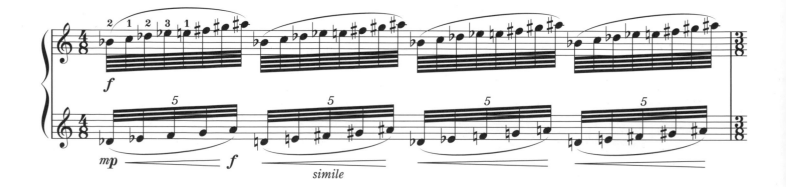

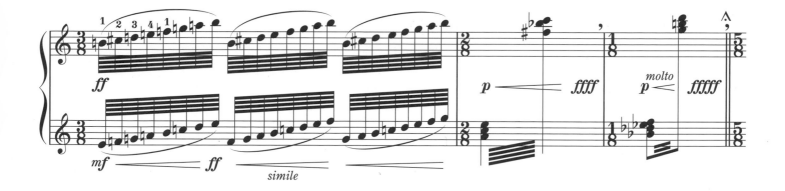

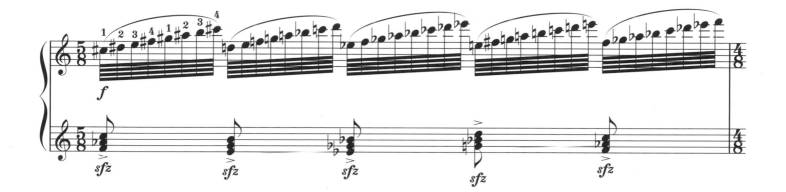

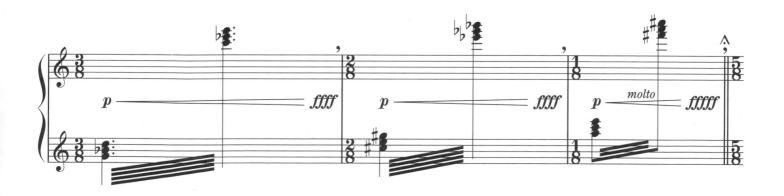

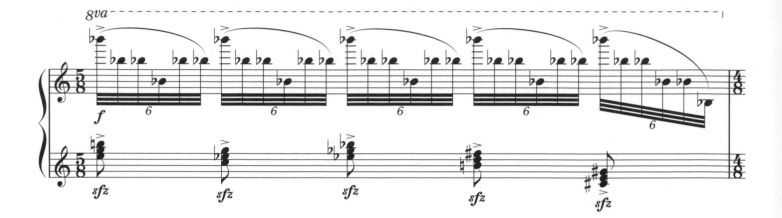

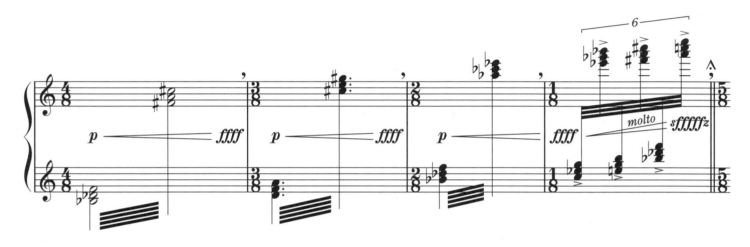

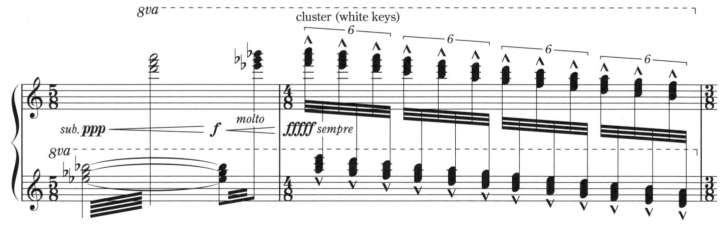

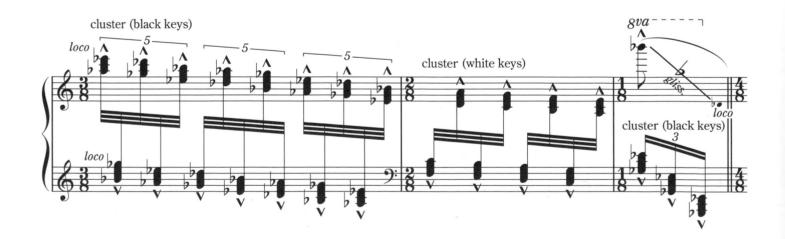

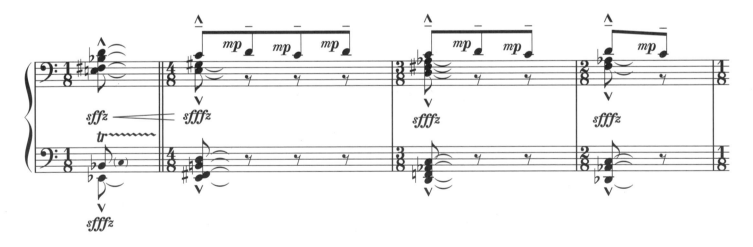

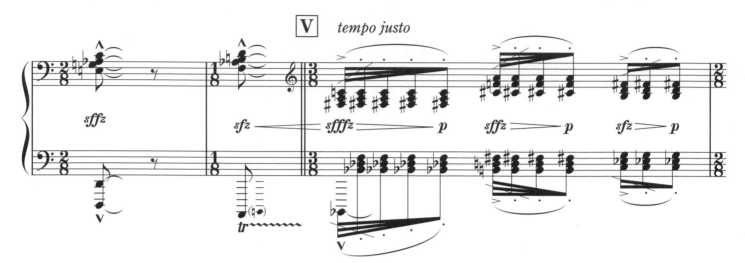

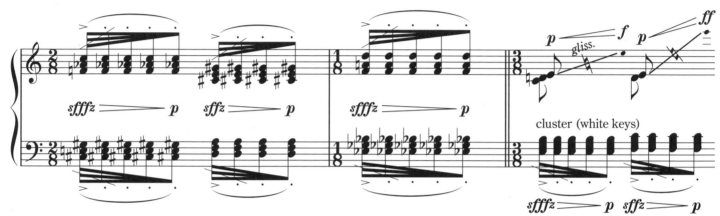

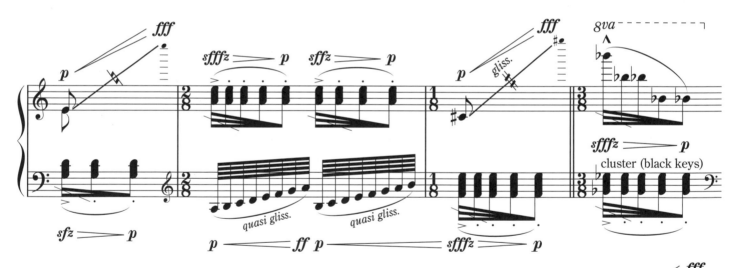

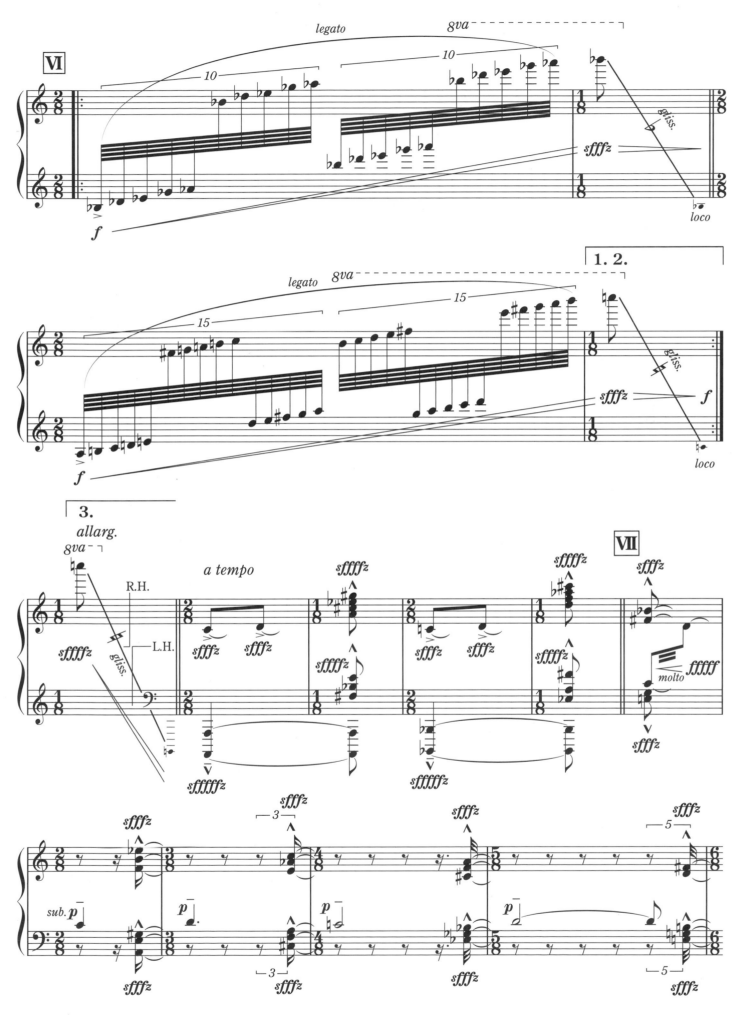

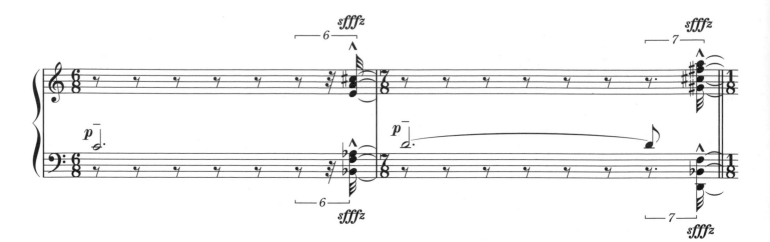

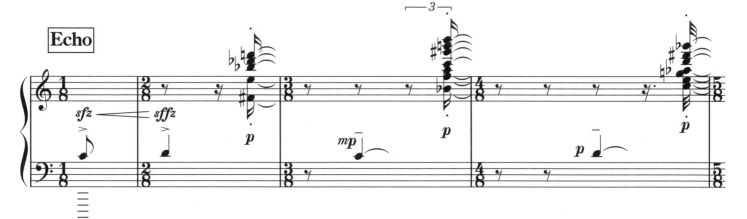

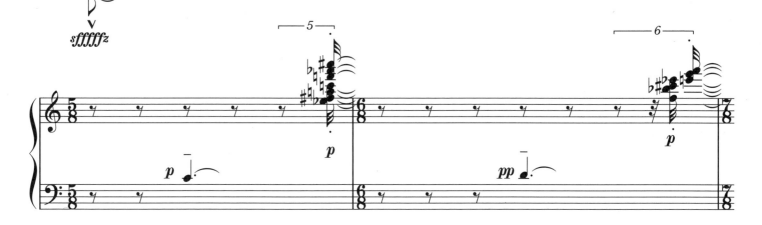

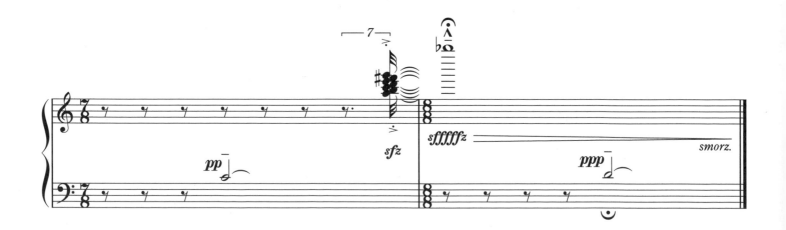

権代敦彦《無常の鐘》　　　　　　　　　●

ピアノのための

初版発行─────────────────2009年2月27日

発行───────────────ショット・ミュージック株式会社

─────────────────東京都千代田区飯田橋2-9-3 かすがビル2階

─────────────────〒102-0072

─────────────────(03)3263-6530

─────────────────http://www.schottjapan.com

─────────────────ISBN 978-4-89066-472-6

─────────────────ISMN M-65001-223-2

現代の音楽
MUSIC OF OUR TIME

権代敦彦   Atsuhiko Gondai (1965–)

十字架の道／光への道
Via Crucis/Via Lucis
for piano . . . SJ 1142 . . . 4200円

武満 徹   Toru Takemitsu (1930–1996)

雨の樹素描
Rain Tree Sketch
for piano . . . SJ 1010 . . . 840円

雨の樹素描 II ──オリヴィエ・メシアンの追憶に──
Rain Tree Sketch II ──In Memoriam Olivier Messiaen──
for piano . . . SJ 1072 . . . 945円

こどものためのピアノ小品とロマンス
『微風』『雲』『ロマンス』
Piano Pieces for Children and Romance
"Breeze" "Clouds" "Romance"
for piano . . . SJ 1123 . . . 1050円

閉じた眼 II
Les yeux clos II
for piano . . . SJ 1056 . . . 1260円

リタニ ──マイケル・ヴァイナーの追憶に──
Litany ──In Memory of Michael Vyner──
for piano . . . SJ 1057 . . . 1260円

湯浅譲二   Joji Yuasa (1929–)

オン・ザ・キーボード
On the Keyboard
for piano . . . SJ 1140 . . . 840円

内触覚的宇宙
Cosmos Haptic
for piano . . . SJ 1138 . . . 840円

内触覚的宇宙II・トランスフィギュレーション
Cosmos Haptic II ──Transfiguration──
for piano . . . SJ 1034 . . . 1050円

プロジェクション・トポロジク
Projection Topologic
for piano . . . SJ 1139 . . . 840円

メロディーズ
Melodies
for piano . . . SJ 1141 . . . 840円

細川俊夫   Toshio Hosokawa (1955–)

ピエール・ブーレーズのための俳句 ──75歳の誕生日に──
"Haiku" for Pierre Boulez ──to his 75th birthday──
for piano . . . SJ 1161 . . . 735円

夜の響き
Nacht Klänge
for piano . . . SJ 1102 . . . 840円

一柳 慧   Toshi Ichiyanagi (1933–)

インター・コンツェルト
Inter Konzert
for piano . . . SJ 1042 . . . 1575円

イン・メモリー・オヴ・ジョン・ケージ
In Memory of John Cage
for piano . . . SJ 1086 . . . 735円

雲の表情 I, II, III
Cloud Atlas I, II, III
for piano . . . SJ 1025 . . . 1050円

雲の表情 IV, V, VI
『IV. 雲の澪』『V. 雲霓』『VI. 雲の瀑』
Cloud Atlas IV, V, VI
"IV. Cloud Vein" "V. Cloud Rainbow" "VI. Cloud Falls"
for piano . . . SJ 1048 . . . 2100円

雲の表情 VII, VIII, IX
『VII. 雲の錦』『VIII. 久毛波那礼』『IX. 雲の潮』
Cloud Atlas VII, VIII, IX
"VII.Cloud Brocade" "VIII. Cloud in the Distance" "IX. Cloud Current"
for piano . . . SJ 1059 . . . 1470円

雲の表情 X
『X. 雲・空間』
Cloud Atlas X
"X.Cloud in the Space"
for piano . . . SJ 1122 . . . 1050円

想像の風景
Imaginary Scenes
for piano . . . SJ 1093 . . . 1365円

ピアノ・スペース
Piano Space
for piano . . . SJ 1145 . . . 1050円

ピアノ・ポエム
Piano Poem
for piano . . . SJ 1147 . . . 1050円

二つの存在
Two Existence
for two pianos . . . SJ 1004 . . . 1050円

ショット・ミュージック株式会社
東京都千代田区飯田橋2-9-3 かすがビル2階　〒102-0072
電話 (03) 3263-6530　ファクス (03) 3263-6672
sales@schottjapan.com　http://www.schottjapan.com

SCHOTT MUSIC CO. LTD.
Kasuga Bldg., 2-9-3 Iidabashi, Chiyoda-ku, Tokyo 102-0072
Telephone: (+81)-3-3263-6530　Fax: (+81)-3-3263-6672
sales@schottjapan.com　http://www.schottjapan.com

（価格には消費税5%が含まれています）